ZANZIBAR to CHICAGO

A BOHRA MUSLIM'S SEARCH FOR GOD

by

Fakhruddin Muhammedali Adamji

ACARA PUBLISHING
HARBERT, MICHIGAN

ISBN: 978-1515248286

to Mary, David, Jehan, Joseph,
My parents and Zanzibar

Acknowledgments

Foremost, I thank my son Joseph and his fiancée Maggie for planting the idea to write this narrative of my life and the impact of its events upon my understanding of religion.

I also thank:

My sister-in-law, Joan Butler, for typing my first draft on the computer so that I could subsequently keep working on it;

My brother-in-law, Fred Kerr, for editing my first draft;

My brother-in-law, Dan Daley, for his enthusiastic support and encouragement to keep writing for an audience beyond my immediate family;

Nadine Kennedy Johnson, our teacher, and my workshop group at Story Studio for their input and encouragement;

Several Bohra friends from Zanzibar who have helped and encouraged me in writing this memoir;

Professors and friends—Terry Rynne, John MacAloon, Roger Myerson and Mohammed Virjee for their feedback and encouragement.

My friend and colleague Dr. Ashok Ray for his companionship and loving support in my journey.

And most of all, my sister-in-law, Kathleen Daley, for her laborious, selfless, repeated readings and editing to the finish.

The Qur'anic quotes are from the 1966 edition of the translation of Holy Qur'an by S.V. Mir Ahmed Ali.

The Gita quotes are from the interpretation of Bhagavad Gita by Swami Prabhupada.

Map of Tanzania

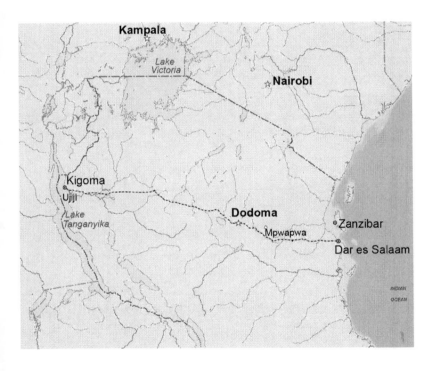

1

Bohras

THE BAND STOOD STILL, ALERT. It waited for the bandleader to give the signal to play the British National Anthem, followed by the Bohra National Anthem. In the blistering heat of the tropical noonday sun, the air was not moving, as if the whole world was at a standstill, waiting. A couple of crows hovered lazily above us and an occasional pigeon flapped its wings on the steps leading to our school.

Suddenly our scoutmaster moved over to whisper something in the ear of the bandleader who promptly commanded us to stand easy. We all relaxed. I was 19 then, the year was 1963, and the place was the Bohra school compound in Zanzibar, a small Indian Ocean island on the east coast of Africa.

Later I heard that the entourage of the Bohra Dai, *Maulana Sayyidena Tahir Seiffuddin* (Maulana for short), was delayed because it had to pause in an alley in Stone Town[1]

---

1   The commercial area of Zanzibar where all immigrants lived

when an elderly Bohra lady fainted in front of the motorcade while running to touch the holy car.

Finally the motorcade, decorated with colorful streamers, arrived at the *Bohra Jamaat Khana*[2] and a small, fair, angelic, bearded figure stepped out, dressed in flowing white robes and turban. The band broke the silence and started playing the National Anthem and the Bohra men and women burst out crying and shouting, *"Allaho Akber."*[3] The Maulana raised his frail white arm; it seemed as if it would never come down. With his arm still raised he was gently escorted into the Jamaat Khana and the flocks hurried restlessly to get a glimpse of his face, touch his hands and feet, and, of course, listen to his sermon.

Soon the festivities began. We, the Bohra scouts, planned to parade through the streets of Stone Town, the band leading us. "Left, right, left right, left, right, left," echoed loudly in the maze of narrow alleys as we marched in columns. Pedestrians stopped to watch us, sometimes bracing their backs against the walls of the alleys to let us pass by; women peaked through doors and windows, and children joined us in front, behind, and all around. After the parade on foot we paraded on bicycles in the outskirts of the town. In the evening the troop organized entertaining events for the community—plays and songs of praise for the beloved holy visitor.

The Dai is to Daudi Bohras as the Pope is to Catholics; he is the spiritual head of all the Bohras in the world. Never before, since the arrival of Bohras in East Africa in the mid-nineteenth century, had any Dai set foot in East Africa. Therefore this was a great historic event for which the Bohra School was closed, businesses were shut down and Bohra professionals took time off work.

---

2 Community center
3 God is Great

Whereas it was a festive time for all Bohras, it was a very memorable time for me personally. That year I had been chosen to be the troop leader and as troop leader I got to carry the Union Jack at the front of the parade in the day time, and to lead the singing of songs of praise for our Maulana in the evening. However, I had to work hard at hiding the doubt and the guilt festering within me then. I was having a serious "lovers' quarrel" with my God for reasons that will become apparent later.

I found the pomp and show of the visit and the servile attitude my community elders maintained towards the religious leaders rather inappropriate. Spirituality embodies and exemplifies simplicity; this visit did not. But I dared not share my views with many people lest I become unpopular. My father and my friends reminded me that our leaders were the glue for our community, a very well-organized worldwide community that provided us security, shelter, and a rich community life in all corners of the world.

Only one million in number, we were a minority immigrant community wherever we lived. Therefore our worldwide institution gave us strength. The Dai was our Prophet's representative on the Earth and we worshipped him as a savior in difficult times. So often I heard my mother invoke his name when she felt anxious or stressed. A photograph of his figure praying on a mat or bowing to a lion or a tiger he had shot in the African wild hung in every Bohra household.

The Bohras are just one sect among several congregations of Indians living in Zanzibar. Each group is defined by its religious affiliation: a scattering of Christians mainly from Goa, a large group of Hindus consisting of several castes, and a large community of Muslims made up of Sunnis and three divisions of Shiites, *Ismaili Khojas*,[4] *Ithna'ashari Khojas* and

---

4   The most progressive of the three

the *Bohras*. There were a handful of Parsi Indians[5] and a few families of Ceylonese Buddhists as well.

Each group of Indians had its own place of worship, its own parochial school, its own gymnasium called gymkhana, and its own cemetery. We did not intermarry much, and apart from competing in sports, we did not participate in cultural events. It was as if each group lived in an exclusive compound in which its members were born, worshipped and died. But we lived together in Stone Town, in homes that were scattered all over randomly, fully respecting our differences.

All Indians were immigrants from the northwest corner of India and most of us were Guajarati. Although, throughout history, migration and trade diversified the populations living in the coastal lands of the Indian Ocean, the Persian Gulf and the Red Sea (a body of water the Greeks called the Erythraean Sea), the largest migration of Indians occurred after 1880 when East Africa became a British Protectorate. The British invited us to go there because the British had already taught us their ways in India. They had ruled India for 200 years. We knew their law, their language and their trade. We bought and sold only British goods. Therefore we were good for the British Empire's interests in East Africa.

Until 1880 the Sultan of Oman ruled East Africa. Before him the Portuguese established a stronghold there to protect the trade route to India. All these powers traded in ivory, rhinoceros horn, spices, gold, and most importantly, slaves captured on the mainland. The Arabs were heavily involved in the slave trade, a fact that came to haunt all of us one day.

The Arabs, the Europeans (mainly the British), and a few very wealthy Indians lived in the more wealthy areas on the periphery of Stone Town.

The majority of Africans, as fishermen or farmers on the

---

5   Persians who had settled in India

land that was mostly owned by Arabs and a few Indians, lived in villages outside the town.

The island was about forty miles long and twenty miles wide and its total population was about three hundred thousand. Ninety-nine percent of the population was Muslim.

The Band

The Parade

Bicycle Parade

Entertainment

Young Gandhi and Gokhle in Zanzibar

Bohra School

2
Zanzibar

IT IS A MIRACLE THAT given a simple prompt, the human mind can travel back over decades and thousands of miles in a split second. That is what happened to me a few months ago when my wife Mary and I were visiting our third child, Joseph, and his fiancée Maggie, in Minneapolis. They took us on a mystery walk through alleys and narrow streets lined with restaurants emitting odors of breakfast foods and the sounds of folk music.

We soon came upon the Minneapolis Art Museum, our destination. Navigating a maze of rooms until we came to what looked like a dead end, the kids asked us to slow down and make a sharp turn to the left. As soon as I made the turn, I was struck by what I saw. Standing in the middle of the large room, looking lonesome and out of place, stood an old, rugged, and worn Zanzibar door, a heavy wooden door studded with brass knobs. Flowers, fish and Arabic writing were carved on it. Some fading chalk writing was still legible.

As soon as I saw it, I froze, choked up and was overcome with the urge to touch it and kiss it. Tears welled in my eyes. My wife asked what was wrong, but words failed me. Emerson's words, "Sorrow's Crown of Sorrow is in remembering old things," came to my mind, for the door had opened flood gates of wonderful memories of my life in Zanzibar, almost sixty years ago.

The life of my childhood in Zanzibar was indeed very special. Like the steady and delightful weather of a tropical coral island and the calm waters of the Indian Ocean around it, life on the island had a simple, gentle rhythm to it and the encounters with people were always pleasant, familiar, and predictable.

The Muezzin's call to prayer from the minaret of the nearby Ithna'ashari mosque ushered in the day at dawn. Still lying on my futon bunk bed, making an effort to wake up, I would hear the rustle of my parents and siblings as they were getting ready for morning prayers.

First we had to perform ablutions. Ablution is a ritual of cleaning with water the face, the head, the nose, the ears, the mouth, the arms and feet while uttering specific prayerful words in the name of Allah. The seven of us—my parents, my brother Yusuf, my sisters Shirin and Gulshan, my nephew Hamza and I—shared one bathroom, therefore it took a while before we were all finished.

After ablution, we put on special clothes for prayers: a white robe and a white cap for men and a skirt and a head-covering shawl for women. The routine was so ritualistic that we knew each other's moves and whereabouts and no one spoke.

By the time I was ready, the aroma of incense wafted through the house and my mother would already be sitting in her favorite corner, on a mat, facing east towards Mecca, reading the Qur'an or rolling the beads on her rosary. I walked with my father, my brother and Hamza to the mosque, about fifty yards down the street and around the corner to the left. We would meet and whisper greetings to other Bohras sauntering in.

Taking off our shoes or sandals at the doorstep, we would enter the dim, quiet space inside the mosque, spread our mats in our favorite spots—elders in front, youngsters in the back—and wait for the arrival of the Imam, the mullah who would lead us in prayer. When he arrived, softly greeting us on his way with "*assalaam-o-alaikum,*"[1] he would go straight to his vestibule, the place in front designated for imams.

After a few minutes of meditation he would signal us to line up in rows behind him and commence the prayer. Following his cues, we prayed in unison, like all Muslims do. All the words uttered in prayers are in Qur'anic Arabic and it did not matter that we did not understand any of the words; all that mattered was that we listened attentively, repeated the words correctly and performed the rituals of the prayer correctly. There was no sermon, no announcements, and no music.

Once the prayer session was over, in about twenty minutes, we queued up in front of the Imam to perform the ritual of *salaam*, which is a very revered way of exchanging good wishes of peace and love with one another. It is initiated by a younger person when greeting an older person or a brother when greeting a sister. The initiator holds the right hand of the person he is greeting with both hands, touches it

---

1   peace be upon you

with his or her right eye, the left eye, the forehead, and finally the lips, then kisses the hand.

At the mosque, after prayers, the imam stands in the vestibule and the oldest among us goes first to perform the salaam greeting to the imam. Once finished he stands next to the imam and then the rest follow, with the elders first and the youngest last. Thus we wish peace and love to every person gathered for the prayers.

We dispersed quietly and went home to my mother and sisters who would also have finished their prayers at home. (Except for holy days, women preferred not to get dressed and walk to the mosque for daily prayers.) We performed salaams to them as well. We all felt good for having prayed and having greeted one another.

After changing clothes, my father went swimming in the Indian Ocean, only a seven-minute walk from our house. He would ask me to join him if I was not going with my friends or with my nephew Hamza.

After swimming we came home for the breakfast prepared by my mother usually consisting of an egg, a leftover curry dish from the previous day, sweetened cream from boiled milk, toasted bread and tea.

For all the meals of the day, we ate together, sitting on mats on the floor around a large round metal plate resting on a wide metal ring, as now we do at Ethiopian restaurants. The food rested on the big round plate for common sharing; there were no individual plates. We drank water from one glass passed around as needed. Soda was too expensive and alcohol was not allowed for religious reasons. We drank only tap water at room temperature. We had no refrigerator.

As was common for all our activities, a specific ritual accompanied our meal. Heads had to be covered (hats for men and shawls for women), a pinch of salt was passed around at the beginning, and an elder pronounced *Bismillahir Rahmaanir Rahim*[2] as the signal that we could commence eating. Conversation was minimal, my mom asking everyone what his or her pleasure was for lunch or my father describing the tide or announcing events in the community that day. Never was there any political conversation nor was there any gossip. To gossip was to sin.

With breakfast over, we were ready to step into the world outside. By this time the streets and alleys had begun to buzz and pulse with the life of the island. People walked or rode bicycles. There were no cars.

A walk through Stone Town was like a walk through an Oriental Bazaar, a cornucopia of sensual delights. Two doors down the street from my house was a Sheria hotel (the Sheria were Arabs from Muscat), blasting Egyptian and Taarab music (orchestral music of Zanzibar), serving spicy tea, sweet fried bread, curried goat, and dried fish brought by sailors from across the Indian Ocean. Arab and African men dressed in long flowing skirts and white caps embroidered with gold-colored thread and shaped like the Turkish fez, shuffled in and out of the hotel. Black sandals carved out of recycled tires were fashionable footwear.

Walking through the serpentine alleys, in and out of the tropical sun and the shade of the corrugated tin roofs on the whitewashed sandstone buildings attached to one another, I inhaled the ocean breeze filled with the smell of curry, garlic, asafetida, incense and the aromatic oils worn by women and men alike. I was bombarded by the cacophonous sounds of Indian music, English music, Taarab music and Egyptian music, and the voices of school children singing the alphabet, bicycle bells, the clock bells of Big Ben, Christian church bells and Hindu temple bells. Still I would not fail to hear the

---

2   in the name of the merciful God

wailing of the Muslim muezzin reminding everyone that it was time for prayer.

God was ever present amongst us.

Flattening your back against the wall of the alley to avoid getting run over by a wooden cart carrying cargo from a ship, or stepping aside for a bicycle carrying a large basket of fruit or a keg of milk for home delivery, you would feel welcome and perfectly comfortable amongst the medley of people of various shades of brown and black dressed in white and colorful clothes, going about their business, chatting, smiling, laughing, shouting, greeting and walking languorously. For the islanders, time was not a commodity.

As a tourist, losing your way was never an issue, for any one of these men would be happy to help you. An encounter with a foreigner, especially if he were a European with colorful hair, colorful eyes, and rose-colored, sun-burned exposed legs and arms, carrying a camera or two, conjured up in our minds images of the freedom, great wealth and exciting cultures of faraway lands. We loved it. The Indian shopkeeper sitting in a wooden chair outside his shop, reading a newspaper or a holy book, would be more than happy to offer a glass of water and strike up a conversation. Wide-eyed, smiling, laughing groups of children would be thrilled to show you around town, just so that they could boast to their families and friends of their adventure.

If you were lucky, you could run into a school teacher on his way from school for siesta, a teacher like my father —a short, stocky, clean-shaven, white-haired man. A Jina cap (the kind shown in his photograph below), a pleasant smile, a starched white shirt buttoned up to his neck, a starched khaki pair of trousers with a few patches sewn by my mother on her Singer sewing machine, and polished, brown, weather-beaten leather shoes gave away the simple, pleasant, and humble personality of one who was comfortable with himself. He carried books in one hand while he greeted his former students in their shops with the other. He would be happy to talk to you and show off his King's English. Jokingly he might even tease you with "Have you been to London to see the Queen?" for the English Queen was our queen too and we loved the British.

Hard, however, it would be to strike up a conversation with the African and Arab women passing by, wearing brightly colored *khangas* underneath their black *Bui Bui* which covered them from head to foot. Or with the Indian lady with a gold pin in her nose, a red dot on her forehead, in a colorful sari, holding it at her neck to make sure it did not slide off her head, floating by you with ankle bracelets jingling. Women in Zanzibar shied away from talking to strangers in the streets.

As you strolled around, avoiding pot holes filled with rain water or a beggar paralyzed below the waist sitting with a collection box by his side, you would notice shop after shop after shop selling groceries, spices, clothing, utensils, hardware, sporting goods, bicycles. Interspersed here and there were small hotels where you could go for a meal any time of the day and fruit stalls where you could pick up local and imported fruit. Once in a while you would run into a *paanwala* shop where Indian men with stained teeth gather to while away the time. They chat and crack jokes while they chew a *pan*[3] and then spit into a corner every few minutes. You would not miss the coffee man wearing a red fez, a white skirt and a khaki jacket carrying a conical charcoal grill in one hand. On top of the grill would be a brass pot brewing fresh coffee. In the other hand he would hold a bunch of Turkish coffee cups that he jingles with a flourish every so often to announce his coming around, perhaps for a second or third

---

3   a wrap of a leaf filled with tobacco and beetle nuts

time down the same street. He was quite a fixture.

And of course you would notice the famous Arab, Zanzibar doors. The kind of door I mentioned at the beginning of this chapter. They are everywhere, big heavy wooden doors studded with shiny, pointed brass knobs and decorated with designs of flowers, leaves, fish and Qur'anic script carved by Persian, Indian and Arab artisans in faraway places. They were imported long ago for the homes of rich Arabs.

Wearing my school uniform—a white shirt, khaki shorts, white shoes and socks—and sporting on my right shoulder a satchel, locally made from palm leaves and filled with books, I would walk to the Bohra Primary School, only 200 yards up the street from my house on Saxi Street. The school was one of the largest buildings in Stone Town, three stories tall with high ceilings, an Arab building that used to be a subsidiary slave market, so the story goes. It had a large, open compound in front (used to dry cloves in the old days), where I loved to play with my many friends. We played games like pickup cricket, "iti danda,"[4] and even *hututu*, a uniquely Indian game. It is played standing and running around one another while muttering "hututu" in one breath. One of my favorites was "gomay." It is a game like baseball, played with a tennis ball and a fist for a bat.

Sometimes we simply hung out there. Boys did not mix with girls. Girls had their own games to play, like hopscotch, skipping rope and hide-and-seek. Only Bohra boys and girls went to this school that went from first to eighth grade. Girls wore a uniform consisting of a long blue skirt, white trousers and a thin shawl to cover the head and upper body. The classrooms for girls and boys were separate but the subject matter taught was the same, except perhaps for male and female hygiene.

4   an Indian game played with sticks

The language of instruction was Gujarati since Bohras come from Gujarat. Major subjects were English, arithmetic, Gujarati and religion. There were three religion lessons every day; one lesson about how to read the Qur'an (our Bible) correctly, in Arabic, with proper pronunciation, one to learn how to perform the rituals of prayers and ablution correctly and one on proper Muslim conduct.

Many years passed before it occurred to me how strange it was that we were not taught either Arabic or Kiswahili, two languages that played such an important role in our lives. Our religion is an Arabic religion. Our Dai is a Yemeni by heritage. We spent much time and effort learning how to pray in Arabic and recite the Quran, written in Arabic, yet we did not learn what it all meant. And Kiswahili was important because we were living in a land of Swahili people, not only in Zanzibar but all over East Africa.

My father walked to Smith Madressa School, a public school, funded by the British Government, where he taught sixth-, seventh-, and eighth-grade English, arithmetic, and geography. Hindu, Sunni Muslim and Ithna'ashari boys studied there. Because he taught non-Bohra boys, my father got exposure in those communities, as a result of which he acquired many non-Bohra friends. Through these friends he learned much about non-Bohra cultures.

He was a gentle, mild and soulful man who loved children. "You must learn to laugh at yourself," he frequently preached to us kids. He loved to be teased. He taught each of us how to ride a bicycle, swim, and play cricket among other things. He was a "curve baller" for his cricket team. He was generous and kind, he was genuine in speech and action, and a cheerful calmness about him made everyone love him.

He was a self-made man who never stopped studying. His formal teaching went up to only the fourth grade (the highest grade, I guess, in early twentieth century Zanzibar) but his mind was so curious about the world that he gathered and read books on the ancient Greeks, Romans, Persians, and, of course, the English. He loved to read the classics and collect beautiful writings which he hid from my mother under his mattress, for my mother would make fun of him for reading "strange" books all the time. Shakespeare, Aeschylus, Dickens, and Kipling, to mention only a few, rubbed shoulders on his bookshelf. And of course he read the Qur'an and other Arabic writings, in translation, even though the priests discouraged us from reading translations, lest they were inaccurate. His favorite destination in the evenings was the Zanzibar library, part of the museum near the cricket field on the outskirts of Stone Town. There he read current magazines and newspapers.

All schools on the island had two sessions: a morning session that ended at noon for prayers followed by lunch, and an afternoon session from two to four. Lunch was the main meal of the day. I do not know how much education my mother had but besides being charming and beautiful, she was the best cook I ever knew. She spent most her morning preparing dishes like curry-goat, curry-fish, coconut chicken and aromatic rice dishes like biryani and pilaf, not to mention samosas, chapattis and parathas—all Indian dishes with an African-island twist. After a heavy meal like that, a quiet restful siesta was in order.

Four o'clock was a prized time for me. The fond memories of sitting on a mat by our front door with my siblings and my dad, as my mother served us tea and home-cooked snacks while we did our homework, are vivid and cherished memories to this day. I still remember my father reading Robinson Crusoe aloud. After an hour of schoolwork we dispersed, my father walking to the museum library and my nephew Hamza and I to the gymkhana where we played sports such as cricket, volleyball, and table tennis. If we did not go to the gymkhana, we went to the Jubilee Gardens to hang out with our friends. (Hamza was younger so he played with his friends while I hung out with my own very steady pals.)

We went for walks along the oceanfront and watched girls strolling by, watching boys. Often at six o'clock we ran to greet the Sultan coming out of his palace in his shining red Rolls Royce. We would then sit at the edge of the water with our snacks and watch the golden day sink into the bright starry night over the Indian Ocean, leaving us wondering who was waking up on the other side of the globe.

At sunset it was time for prayers again. We went to the mosque if we were in town or we prayed at the gymkhana when we were there.

Dinner was never an elaborate meal. We ate food left over from lunch. The time for dinner varied depending on our activities, but we always waited for everyone to come home so that we could eat together. The time after dinner was a quiet time spent at home doing homework or visiting neighbors. Sometimes we went to the mosque for a gathering of sorts.

Such was a typical day in the life of our family, or any Bohra family for that matter, sessions of prayer with sessions of work or school or leisure in between. Life revolved around the mosque.

Forty years later, thousands of miles away from Zanzibar, when I was exploring other religions in the United States, my new, adopted country, I experienced the same cycle of life when I spent a weekend of retreat with a few Trappist monks living at Mellerey Abbey in Iowa. They gathered for prayer vigils several times a day and when they were not praying, they worked on their farms or in their workshop making coffins that they sold for their livelihood.

Life in our Zanzibar Bohra community, akin to life in a proverbial village, was enchanting to say the least. Everyone knew everyone else. Many families were related to each other through intermarriage. All elders were uncles and aunts to the children even if they were not blood relatives, and the children paid attention to the elders.

I still remember the alley and the day on which, while riding my bicycle, I accidentally ran into a blind man carrying food. He fell and the food spilled to the ground. He simply cursed loudly, got up and started walking away. A Bohra elder sitting outside his shop witnessed the incident and called me. "Fakhru! Come here! Whose fault was that, do you think?" I admitted it was mine. He smiled, patted me, gave me some money and told me to run to the blind man, apologize for my mistake and give him the coins. He then dismissed me, not forgetting to advise me to pay more attention while riding my bicycle.

Not only did we feel connected within the community, we also felt connected to the island community at large because the vast majority of the people were Muslims. With non-Muslims we were simpatico because we all came from the same part of India, Gujarat, and we shared the same culture and language.

There were quite a few occasions when the Muslims of the island got together to celebrate. One such gathering was Maulidi during the month of Rabbiul Awwal, when the Prophet was born. The whole island descended on Mnazimmoja grounds, a large playing field on the outskirts of Stone Town. People from all over the island came dressed in their best clothes to hear sermons and songs of praise for the life and work of the Prophet and to watch the Arabs dancing. Children from all schools were invited to participate in recitals. I remember climbing high up to the podium with my classmates, many a time, to recite verses from the Qur'an or to sing a song in Arabic taught to us at school by our Mullah teacher.

The month of Ramadhan was a special time as well. It was as if the whole population were observing the fasting. A special quiet descended during the day. Shops were closed for a longer time at siesta. People spent more time praying. Sports activities were limited. But after sundown, after the breakfast, the whole island poured out into the streets, lit up and filled with the usual sounds and smells. People gathered on street corners just to talk, or went to the Jubilee Gardens, emblazoned with hundreds of candles and teaming with hawkers and venders selling fruits and finger foods galore while the loud speakers hanging from trees blasted verses from Al Qur'an or Taarab music.

At the end of the month there were four days of festival at Mnazimmoja grounds. (Today, American summer festivals always remind me of those Idd festivals). Festival time was one of my favorite times. Children dressed in fancy clothes would pay visits to the relatives and friends of their parents, greet them with the salaam greeting and have a personal conversation with the elder, one to one. The elder would inquire of each about how he or she was doing, especially in schoolwork. The children would then be given a small gift of pocket money before they walked on to the next relative or friend. I loved my aunts and uncles and I knew they loved me too.

It was a good life. It was a simple life. We were at peace within, we were at peace without. It seemed as if life was always lived that way; it seemed as if it would always be that way. We were like cattle, grazing contentedly in rich peaceful pastures on an enchanting coral island, unaware of the world beyond.

"Contentment is better than wealth," my father wrote on one of his pieces of paper, "it is a reservoir that never dries up," he added, copied from a Greek play or one of the many proverbs of Maulana Ali, I suspect.

But he failed to observe that contentment can put a people to sleep! And it did.

Someday I would reminisce with my children, quoting Mr. Dickens, that in Zanzibar, of that time, "we had everything before us; we had nothing before us."

Saxi Street

Jubilee Garden

3
Doubt

ONE DAY IN 1950 MY *fuwaaji*, a paternal uncle, called me and said, "Fakhru, come here! Watch how Doctor Patel is dressing the wound on my leg. I want you to do the same for me tomorrow."

I was six years old then, visiting and playing with his stepson, my cousin Qurban, in a small alley in Mkunazini. This is what I tell my friends in America when they ask me about how and when I decided to become a doctor.

Doctor Patel was everyone's doctor in the Stone town, or so it seemed to me. He was of average build but very fair for an Indian. Not only was he good looking, he made sure he wore clothes and a pair of glasses that suited him. Whenever I saw him in the streets, he was walking with his usual confident step, carrying his doctor's bag, but he never appeared to be in a hurry. I never saw him talking loudly to anyone; he whispered even when he greeted someone, and he always greeted people with an inviting smile. If he stopped somewhere for a reason, people around him stood up to see if he needed anything.

We never saw him in Stone Town except when he was going to visit a patient. Many times I saw him walking and playing with his brown and white Springer spaniel on the golf course on the outskirts of the town. He was the only Indian I knew who had his own dog. I guessed he lived and spent his leisure time on the periphery of Stone Town where the rich people lived. I watched him secretly from afar whenever he was around in Stone Town and many a time I walked up to him just to invite his response to my greeting. I adored Dr. Patel. He was very special to all of us. I thought all doctors were like him.

My uncle was a very rich moneylender, and according to my father, he was so rich that you could walk from sunrise to sunset in a straight line and still be on his land. But he was as stingy as he was rich. Since he did not want to pay one shilling to the doctor for his services, he wanted me to dress his leg instead. I observed the doctor and learned how to clean my uncle's sore and dress it daily. When the healing showed signs of progress, my uncle started addressing me as "Dr. Fakhru" and soon my family did the same. I was very proud and flattered by the title of "doctor." I decided to grow up to be one, just like Dr. Patel. That meant that in eighth grade I had to do well in the examination in order to enter the coveted government secondary school, which in turn meant that I had to study very hard. And study hard I did.

However, before I was ten years old, a very pretty but strange teenage girl from the big city of Dar-es-Salaam joined our family. This is how it transpired. My 21-year-old brother, having just finished secondary school (high school in the American system of education) wanted to go to England for "further studies," to become a professional. But my parents felt that since jobs were available in Zanzibar and they were afraid that he would be lost to them in England, he should get a job and settle in Zanzibar. He did as they wished and soon they arranged a marriage for him.

What I am about to describe is an example of how marriages occurred in our society in those days. It may still happen in some families. Mullahs (like deacons in a Christian church) enjoy a very respectful and sometimes powerful position in the Bohra community. Such a mullah named Mullah Ibrahim lived in the big city of Dar-es-Salaam on the coast of Tanganyika, about twenty miles away from Zanzibar across the Zanzibar Channel. Dar-es-Salaam is much bigger, more developed and more westernized than Zanzibar.

Our family had never gone there and we did not know anyone living there. We had never heard of Mullah Ibrahim. But my maternal uncle, whose name was also Ibrahim and who lived two doors down from us in Zanzibar, knew Mullah Ibrahim through business connections. Mullah Ibrahim had a daughter who was about fourteen or fifteen. In retrospect, I think she was not an easy child and she gave him reason to worry. He thought that her spirits would settle down if she got married. Therefore Mullah Ibrahim asked my Uncle Ibrahimji to suggest to my parents that they marry my twenty-one-year-old brother to the Mullah's daughter.

My parents saw no reason to object; after all, the girl came from a Mullah's family; she must be well-trained and respectable. So after a short period of engagement, our entire extended family, including my uncles and aunts, went to Dar-es-Salaam for the wedding.

I had a great deal of fun travelling across the Zanzibar Channel in a steamboat called Sayed Khalifa (the Sultan's name) and walking around with my cousins in a city with big buildings and big boulevards teaming with cars. Most of all, I was very excited about acquiring a beautiful new sister who would come to live with us.

But the fun did not last very long. The teenager could not and did not wish to try to adjust to living in our family, in a town smaller and very different from hers. She did not wish to learn anything from my mother who tried her best to teach her how to cook and perform household chores. She kept flying to Dar-es-Salaam, spending weeks with her parents. After all she was only a teenager and must have been homesick.

She would argue with my mother over petty things and treated my gentle sister Shirin, who was her age, mercilessly—ignoring her and calling her names—to the point of making my sister cry. At meals my mother began to give my sister-in-law more attention than she gave to us, purposely, to make her feel very special. But the girl could not be satisfied.

In our culture, the wife of the oldest son is held in high esteem and enjoys a privileged position second to the mother. Therefore, my sister-in-law's disapproval of our family made the child in me suspect that we were unlikable people; that I was unlikable. It was a doubt that had never crossed my mind before she came, a heavy shackle that dragged me down until I was released one distant day, one fourth of July, many years later, in a faraway place inhabited by strangers.

The tension in the family kept mounting as weeks and months passed. My mother began to suffer from stress and depression. Her beautiful easy smile was replaced by a forced grin. Silence and tension displaced spontaneous conversation. Coming home after school and after playing outside became so unpleasant and depressing for me that I started taking long, solitary walks, or I rode my bicycle to Mtoni, a fishing village about four miles out of town, to while away my time on the lonely beach.

Eventually my brother, realizing that the marriage was doomed, suggested to my parents that he should divorce his wife. But by now a child had arrived. So, like all Bohras in general, living in fear of other people's opinions and gossip, my mother feared that our family name would be tarnished for having ruined a young girl's life. My mother did not agree to divorce. She spent all her energy and time trying to win the girl over but to no avail. And the tension in the family kept growing. Finally it became so unbearable that my brother decided to separate from the family and live on his own with his wife and son. I lost my brother then, for he saw less and less of all of us after that.

These were very difficult times for all of us, but the rituals of going to the mosque, taking part in community events, going to work or school, doing our duty, kept us afloat.

The seeds of my quarrel with my parents and my religious community were planted. I was angry with my parents for having put my brother in such a predicament. His wife was not his choice and when he wanted to end his relationship with her, they did not let him because of the pressures of our society. Because I loved my parents a lot, I could not sustain that anger. I blamed our culture instead. I did not want to be part of it anymore.

I buried myself in my schoolbooks, determined to get into King George VI Secondary School, and I did. The school provided me with an escape. My classmates, all very bright and interesting, came from a cross section of all the communities on the island. My teachers came from England, America, India, and the Comoro Islands, in addition to a few from Zanzibar.

The study of English took me to the England of Charles Dickens, Joseph Conrad, Shakespeare, and others. The study of history and geography took me to far away countries and nations of the world. Physics took me to the cosmic world of the heavens. And biology, especially Darwin, raised exciting questions about the origin and evolution of life in general and of mankind in particular, thus raising serious questions about the truths propagated by the Holy Books and the religious authorities. After six years—four years of secondary and two years of high school (junior college in the American system)—I was clearly thinking outside the box that was our religion and our view of life.

4

Relief

THE VISIT OF THE DAI (the one I opened this story with) in 1963 lasted for many days. Great celebrations ensued with feasting and *Majlis*.[1] Group youth initiation services (*Mishaq*), group weddings and group graduation to Mullahood (priesthood) took place, all for a nominal fee.

Throughout those days, the community buzzed with the news that miracles had occurred. One miracle, which everybody, including the elders, walked miles in the hot sun to witness, occurred in the garden of the mansion of the rich family who had hosted the holy entourage. A tomato had grown on one of the plants with letters "*Ya Ali*" inscribed on it. *Ya* means "oh" and *Ali* is the founder of the Shia religion. On examining the tomato and understanding what had been done, I felt angry and disgusted at whoever had played such a cheap joke on the community. Obviously a young child had written those words on the green tomato but the community seriously thought it was a miracle.

Also arranged during that time were visitations; every family was welcome to invite the Maulana or his son to their home, to have it blessed by the Holy Spirit (for a nominal fee). To my surprise, my brother, who I felt was not rich enough to afford it, arranged for such a visit by Maulana's son. As members of my brother's family, we were given the chance to touch and kiss his holy hands—salaam him and get blessed. He was dressed in a white robe and a white turban. Standing in a corner of a second floor room of my brother's house in Mkunazini, humbly, quietly, he received citizens' greetings and blessed them, one by one.

When my turn came, I stepped up to him, nervously, and reached forward to hold his hand. But all I could touch were his fingers, which he appeared to withdraw quickly from my fingers before I could properly finish the salaam ritual. I felt a cold shiver go down my spine, worried that perhaps he suspected my lack of devotion to the faith.

As soon as the holy visit was over, I buried myself in my books again, in preparation for my Cambridge High School Certificate examinations.

At that time, the U.S. space program had set up a satellite tracking station in Zanzibar and in appreciation had offered eight scholarships to qualified students to study in America. To qualify we had to pass the SAT examination.

Therefore after the departure of our Dai, I took the English HSC examination as well as the SAT. Then I waited. I found temporary employment at a government office as a filing clerk and I volunteered to teach at our grammar school.

Close to the end of that year I received the welcome news that I had done well in the SAT examination and that I was one of the eight students to receive the U.S. scholarship. I would be promptly notified about when to report to the U.S. Embassy for the official reception. To celebrate my accomplishment my mother ordered ice cream for us that evening.

Parents

British Officers, Sultan Abdulla and Abeid Karume (leader of ASP)

5

Upheaval

SOON AFTER WE HAD CELEBRATED the visit of our Maulana, in December 1963, we experienced yet another but bigger celebration. This time the whole island prepared for it—for the independence of Zanzibar from British rule. At midnight, December 12, 1963, the Union Jack was lowered from a white flagpole at Mnazimmoja[1] to be replaced by a flag of the new nation of Zanzibar.

The Zanzibar National Party (ZNP), a predominantly Arab-dominated Party, formed the new government. Six months earlier, the ZNP had won the election, defeating the African-dominated Afroshirazi Party (ASP), a black people's party, simply put. But the ASP was not happy with the way the election had been conducted. They suspected foul play.

A month after the Independence Celebration, on a quiet Saturday night, when my friends and I had returned from the Sultana Cinema which was showing *Ben Hur*, we

---

1   A large cricket field

heard firecracker noises, a very unusual sound in Zanzibar in the middle of the night. But we did not think much of it. However, when we woke up in the morning, we were shocked by loud shouts warning us not to go out of our houses and to shut our doors and windows; there was gun fighting on the island. Sure enough, we heard the loud thumping of heavy footsteps scurrying up and down our narrow alley. When we peaked out of the slits in our windows, we saw African men in street clothes brandishing their machine guns as they ran up and down.

That was the beginning of a successful three-day Communist revolt by a few trained revolutionaries, led by a self-proclaimed "prophet" named John Okello, a Ugandan from Luanga who had found his way into the Zanzibar police force.

That night, the raging ghost of a slave rose up from the land of Hades, as it were, with a ferocious anger and vengeance stronger than that of Achilles. His mighty sword of wrath recalled the indignities, the cruelty and the violence of centuries of the slave trade conducted by the Arabs. The Sultan of Zanzibar managed to flee the island on the first night, but thousands of Arab men and women were killed. In villages all over the island, they were rounded up and marched to beaches, shot in cold blood, and buried in mass graves. Hundreds were shot while trying to escape in canoes. Children and young women were spared.

Most Indians were spared from physical harm also, but we were in a state of great fear and shock. We had been living in such exclusive comfort in the confinement of our communities that we had been blind to the struggles and needs of the indigenous Africans.

For the three days of the revolt, we locked ourselves in our house with ears glued to the Zanzibar radio station, which blasted hourly progress of the revolution. To keep calm, we prayed a lot. Our parents, having complete faith in God, reassured us that what was happening must be in God's plan and that all would be well. There was no need to panic.

When the dust from the uprising seemed to settle, we cautiously began to venture out into the streets, at first a few doors down and after a week, beyond our neighborhood. Our scout- master called a meeting to organize our volunteering at the refugee camps where the now homeless Arab children and women were camped.

I was assigned to the school where my father taught. It was packed with Arab women and children sprawling on the floors in foul-smelling, filthy clothes. We distributed clothes, water, and food to them. Intermittently I saw men, some in street clothes and some in police attire, point to a young Arab woman, grab her hand, and escort her away. She put up no resistance, uttered not a word, her face showing not even fear, her ghostly eyes blankly staring as if at nothing in front of her.

I felt a dagger thrust into my heart as I imagined what the soldier was going to do to the young frightened girl. She had no one to call for help and I dared not reveal my shock at what I was witnessing. The fear, the disgust, the loss of human dignity and trust that I experienced in those days dug such a deep and dark grave in my heart that I have not been able to fill it, even to this day.

My desire to run away from the island picked up urgency. I was ecstatic when I received the invitation to show up at the US Embassy to receive my scholarship. For such an auspicious occasion, I washed and painted my white canvas shoes, my mother ironed my white shirt and khaki pants, cracked her knuckles on my forehead (a gesture of good luck), brushed my hand with scented oil and proudly sent me off.

My whole neighborhood and all my friends knew about that day and they all wished me the best as I hurriedly trotted to the Embassy. A few US officials and my classmates had already gathered and the excitement in the room was palpable. As the hour of the meeting drew nearer, in that hot waiting room with a dark, big, squeaking, and slow-moving ceiling fan, we grew quieter and then waited with charged anticipation for the new Zanzibar government officials to come and accept the gift of scholarships from the US government.

Outside a tropical storm had unleashed a heavy downpour with thunder and lightning. Word came that the officials were delayed. Finally, after long past the designated hour, a Mr. Patterson entered, looked at each of us in turn and somberly announced that the Revolutionary Government of Zanzibar was not interested in receiving any aid from the US or any other capitalist government.

A wide-open door of a great and wonderful opportunity had just slammed shut in my face. All of us sat there in a state of shock. The only sound in the room was the hum and the squeaking of the ceiling fan, interrupted by an occasional nervous cough. Then one by one, with heads drooping, we shuffled out into the street, which was soaked with the rainwater still dripping down from the corrugated iron roofs.

Feeling a choking, sinking sensation in my heart and with no interest in talking to anyone, I hurried home to my mother, looking for comfort. She was in the kitchen, sitting as usual on the floor, cooking. I struggled and broke the devastating news to her. Without a stir, she took a fast look at my face, quickly looked down and continued to cook. If she had tears in her eyes, she did not let me see them. Then to comfort my panic, she said,

"Don't worry, son. It must be God's plan that you will not go to America. Other opportunities will come your way, if God wishes. It is a matter of your Kismet."

She reminded me that it was time for noon prayers and that after the prayers I should look forward to a delicious lunch, for she had cooked fried chicken, samosas and biryani, a flavorful aromatic rice dish worthy of a mogul prince's palate.

But I was dying for my father to show up. When I broke the news to him, he also told me not to worry, to be patient. He would go and talk to a member of the Karimjee family, a rich Bohra magnate, and seek help for me.

The weeks that followed were like an eternity. I do not remember what I did. Jobs were no longer available. Then one day my father told me that the Karimjee Jiwanjee family would grant me a scholarship if I could obtain admission to any college or university. My only hope was the Makerere Medical School at the University of East Africa in Uganda. I applied nowhere else.

While I waited for a letter from the Makerere Medical School, one house at a time in Zanzibar Stone Town was boarded up as Indians were packing to leave. The Communist government had confiscated all private property and had taken over the business of import and export. Each shopkeeper was expected to train an African to run his business and take him on board as a partner. Many Hindus who still had ties with India left for India. The Aga Khan, leader of the Ismailis, helped many of them to migrate to England, Canada, or Australia.

The rest of us, those who had taken up Zanzibar citizenship and carried only Zanzibar passports, could go nowhere and were left to fend for ourselves. My brother got a job in a bank in Dar-es-Salaam where he had moved with his wife and family of three children. My parents stayed back. They managed to survive on a small pension of two hundred shillings that my father received from the British Government. My brother might have subsidized him a little. It was a difficult time for us.

After three or four months of anxious waiting, I received the letter of acceptance at the Makerere Medical School in Kampala.

6

Kampala

MAKERERE UNIVERSITY IS BUILT ON a hill on the outskirts of Kampala, a big metropolis built on several hills in Uganda (in those days the richest country of the four countries that made up British East Africa). The medical college and its hospital have their own hill across Mulago valley about half an hour's walking distance from the main campus.

Unlike Zanzibar, the city has a temperate climate, tall commercial buildings, very busy roads full of cars and trucks, and a people who are mostly Christian and speak Bugandan, a language I do not understand. Moreover it is a city that is landlocked, which made me feel very claustrophobic. Nonetheless, being far away from the toxic atmosphere of a Communist revolutionary Zanzibar and far away from the confinement of communal life meant a welcome breath of fresh air for me.

The medical school started full throttle from the first day.

I struggled for quite a few months with how to organize my study time for subjects such as human anatomy, physiology, and biochemistry, all subjects requiring a great deal of reading, understanding and memorizing.

We were a hundred in my class, all outstanding students from schools all over East Africa. As a result I felt very ordinary, a feeling I had hitherto not experienced when it came to being a student. I had always been considered better than average. To make matters worse, a large number of the students came with classmates and friends from different towns all over East Africa and they formed cliques. I was the only one from Zanzibar, which made me feel very alone.

With time, however, I settled into a tolerable daily routine of study and leisure. On weekends I took long walks to the city, about five miles away, with a friend, Onali. He had been in my grammar school in Zanzibar. He was studying English and Library sciences. I joined the cricket team of our dormitory and the mountain climbing club, which arranged trips up Mount Elgon. On religious holy days the Bohra students from all over the campus would gather and go downtown to the mosque in Kampala.

Throughout my stay in medical school my contact with my family was limited partly because I was very occupied with myself and partly because our only means of communication was through handwritten letters. My father wrote to me every month or so. In some ways I dreaded the letters because the news was always rather depressing. By the time I was a senior student, my sister Gulshan had escaped to Dar-es-Salaam overnight in a boat, to avoid a decree by the revolutionary government that Indian girls must marry African boys.

Most of Stone Town was boarded up. Those who could not go to India or Europe had moved to the mainland of Tanganyika. My poor parents, like other Bohras, had to fend for themselves and somehow relocated with their meager belongings to Dar-es-Salaam.

My father had to leave his precious book collection behind. The whole exotic, charming and colorful culture that had evolved over centuries in Zanzibar, a culture that was the only reality I knew, had been dumped into the depths of the Indian Ocean. Our God had forsaken us and it seemed to me that our religious leaders had forsaken us as well. My anger had no bounds. I buried my head in my books.

Living in Kampala at a distance from my community did provide relief. I was struck by how different Kampala was from Zanzibar. Whereas Zanzibar had a Middle Eastern, Arabian-Nights, port culture and ambience to it, Kampala was a big modern western city. People dressed in jackets and ties, walked fast, as if on a mission, without the shouting and laughing and teasing that I was used to in Zanzibar. There were no children just hanging around or playing in the streets. Roads were tarmac, wide boulevards teaming with cars and trucks. Large commercial buildings looked new and rich. Stores were filled with western machinery, vehicles, manikins of European men and women advertising European clothing. Restaurants sold hamburgers, steaks and fries, cigarettes, beer and other alcohol. Instead of the sounds of people, church bells, temple bells and music that filled our ears in Zanzibar, there was a constant noise of cars, trucks and construction in the streets of Kampala. Whereas Zanzibar had a spiritual atmosphere, Kampala had a commercial atmosphere.

The culture of the campus was liberating and stimulating. The music I heard on campus was Congolese, Lingala, and American Country Music. Jim Reeves was a popular singer. African students walking around on campus with their girlfriends, going to dancing events with them, and drinking alcohol in the dorms were a normal part of the scene. Life of the senses was not taboo. The size, the material richness, the busyness, the sensual stimulation and the cosmopolitan population of the place imparted a carefree feeling. God was not present like he had been in Zanzibar and if he was, he was not obtrusive. Although I felt anonymous, a little odd and old-fashioned, nonetheless I was beginning to love the scene. Its feeling of liberation was very inviting.

In my senior year I did drink a beer or two at the end of my walk to town with Onali. In my dormitory I occasionally bummed a cigarette from a friend. I was beginning to feel unafraid of the God of my childhood.

I was glad when the five years of medical school were over. I went to Dar-es-Salaam, the capital of Tanzania, to do a rotating internship. I enjoyed the practice of medicine, I liked being paid a stipend and, most importantly, I was relieved to be living close to my family. Shirin was the only one missing because she had married my brother-in-law Fazel in Nairobi.

Good fortune comes to us in many guises. When I was six years of age, it came to me as a sore on the leg of a parsimonious uncle who called me a doctor; at the age of nine it came to me as a disruptive sister-in-law whose injection into our family drove me madly in search of a life outside my religious community; after high school it came in the guise of a violent revolutionary government which did not accept American aid; and at the end of my internship in Dares Salaam, it came to me through a random conversation with my colleagues who were talking about a test they had just taken.

The U.S. government, they said, was recruiting physicians. In order to qualify to work in the U.S. we had to pass a test entitled ECFMG—Educational Commission for Foreign Medical Graduates. Even though I had no interest in migrating to the U.S., my friends convinced me to take the test. It cost nothing and it might come in handy someday. Soon after I passed the test I received a "green card" from the U.S., a permit to migrate and work in America. Not being interested in migrating, I filed it away along with my medical certificates. I was bent on living and working in Tanzania and taking care of my parents, my siblings and their children.

Mulago Hospital

Mulago Valley

7
Kigoma & Ujiji

HALF OF MY CHILDHOOD DREAM of becoming a doctor was realized; the other half, of becoming a doctor like Dr. Patel going on rounds in Stone Town of Zanzibar, was never to be realized. That Stone Town was erased from the face of the earth, forever. I had no desire whatsoever to go back to its ruins.

My future was a blank page to be filled with whatever I wanted to fill it with. But I had no idea what my options were. We were a defeated people thrown out of what we thought was our homeland. We felt insulted for being thought of as foreigners who were the cause of the poverty in the country. Africa belongs to Africans, we were told, and we were not Africans. Indians should go back to India, they claimed, but many of us had never set foot in India. But we did not argue. We departed quietly, anxiously and fearfully but ready to step in through any door that was open to us as long as it promised to put beans on the table.

I did not expect any help from members of our community. Everyone was struggling. Our religious leaders from India showed up, once in a while, for moral support and to establish new rules of conduct. In order to increase the funds in the treasury for the welfare of the community, the institution introduced simoniacal practices. The titles of "Mullah" and "Sheikh" were for sale. With the titles came some power. Therefore, since only the rich could afford to buy the titles, the power of the community was being transferred into the hands of the rich but not necessarily the learned.

On the positive side, many families who were interested in starting businesses got help from these coffers in the form of interest-free loans; this got them back on their feet. But our family had no business inclinations. I needed to find a job and start earning a living as soon as I could.

The Tanzanian government hired me as a rural general practitioner and assigned me to the district of Kigoma near a town called Ujiji. It is situated on the western border, on the shore of Lake Tanganyika. Ujiji is a fishing village established by Arabs centuries ago. It is where in 1871, under a mango tree, the explorer Henry Morton Stanley found his predecessor David Livingston and pronounced the famous phrase, "Doctor Livingston, I presume." That mango tree has died but a monument has replaced it. (By the way, when he was exploring East Africa, David Livingston lived on the oceanfront in Zanzibar and his dwelling still stands for all to visit.)

With the blessings of my family, I packed a small suitcase and a box filled with my books and boarded the train to Kigoma. The British built this railroad during colonial times. It stretches from the coastline to the western border of the country. A coal-burning engine powers the train and the travel takes two days and two nights. It takes that long because the train makes numerous stops in little towns along the way. It moves so slowly that it was a well-known joke that one can get off the train, urinate and still run to reboard.

The terrain is picturesque, changing from coastal plains to the African Plateau. At every stop hawkers come up to the windows selling boiled eggs, fruit, baked cassava, corn and smoked fish from baskets balanced nonchalantly on their heads. In the dining car one can buy beer, cigarettes and meals served by uniformed attendants. I am sure the British Colonials of the past enjoyed that ride in style, and I came to love that train ride as well.

At the railroad terminal in Kigoma I was greeted and welcomed by a handsome African man, John, who identified himself as the head nurse of the district hospital that was situated between the towns of Kigoma and Ujiji. John would become a good friend over time.

Because my living quarters were not ready, he invited me to stay with his little family until they were completed. Over the next few weeks his family became my family, and his beautiful, smiley and friendly oldest daughter, Hosanna, became my first girl friend whose friendship I cherished throughout my stay in Kigoma.

The government owned my bungalow. It was a long, rectangular, whitewashed, one-floor building with a corrugated tin roof. It was built on rocky ground fifty yards from the lake and two hundred yards from the hospital. (It was actually an extension of the hospital campus.)

The hospital buildings were similarly constructed. Each building housed patients sleeping on cots or on the floor. There was a male ward, a female ward and a pediatric ward. Additional buildings separately housed the laboratory, the surgical room, labor and delivery, and outpatient clinics.

The staff consisted of three doctors (the medical director,

a Pakistani doctor and me), registered nurses (mostly male), nurse aids and orderlies. The male RNs wore white pants and white short-sleeved safari type jackets; female RNs wore striped blue frocks in male wards and striped pink frocks in pediatric and female wards. The orderlies (all male) wore khaki outfits. Doctors and lab personnel wore white coats.

My colleagues and I divided up our duties. While one person did inpatient work—making rounds, doing surgeries, and delivering babies, the others tended to the numerous outpatients. Making rounds every morning was a ritual I will never forget. The whole group of staff assigned to a ward gathered with me at one end of the long ward. We went down one row of patients, and then turned around along the other row. The head nurse presented the case of the patient and the others filled in more information regarding what might have transpired during the night. I would then examine the patient and dictate the course of treatment. We came to know our patients very well, especially the chronic cases. When such a patient died, we felt a part of us die too.

Surgeries were frequent. Hernias, hydroceles, appendicitis, ectopic pregnancies and cesarean sections were common. Chronic ulcers and infectious diseases like malaria, tuberculosis and typhoid were rampant. The worst case I ever saw (of a condition I have not seen since then) was of tetanus. It was frightening to witness a whole musculature go into a severe spasm, causing the body to arch back and stay in spasm.

The work was very challenging, unending and exhausting. But if God is the being to whom we dedicate all our mind, body and spirit, with selfless love, then the hospital was my church, Hippocrates was my prophet, the medical text was my Qur'an and the patient was my god. I had given up my God of Zanzibar. Rather than simply fearing my God and paying my respects to Him, I was constantly serving my new god; and rather than simply reciting The Qur'an without understanding it, I was studiously looking for guidance from my new Qur'an to fulfill my calling. The practice of medicine was my new religion; and the population I served was my community.

During the week, after a busy day at work, I went home, freshened up and had dinner prepared by my houseboy Juma. He cooked simple rice, meat, fish and vegetable dishes fairly well. Everything tasted the same but I enjoyed it. (I have never been a picky eater.) After dinner I read storybooks or surgical texts if I had to perform a surgery the next day.

Kigoma and Ujiji had plenty to offer for fun on weekends. On Saturdays Hosanna would come to fetch me with her girlfriend and the three of us sometimes walked or took a ride on a minibus to Ujiji about five miles away. Since everyone in the two towns came to know me very quickly as their new doctor, the bus drivers usually gave us a free ride.

Ujiji is an ancient fishing village. It was the farthest outpost of the territories of Tanganyika controlled by the Sultan of Oman who ruled from Zanzibar. He sent big parties led by Arab guides all the way to Ujiji to capture slaves and hunt rhinoceros and elephants. Unlike Kigoma, Ujiji is a Muslim village with many small mosques. It reminded me of Zanzibar but I was not drawn to go and pray in the mosques. I did not feel the need to.

Many a time we would go towards Kigoma and stop under an old Baobab tree where a Congolese band gathered people to dance. Like most Africans, having grown up listening to and dancing to African rhythms, Hosanna was a good dancer and she taught me well. When the sun began to set, we would go to Hosanna's house in town and have a meal cooked by her mom. We all felt very comfortable with each other even though the mother did not speak much English, and my Kiswahili was not perfect. Hosanna was so loving that one day I told her I wanted to marry her, but she said she could not marry me because I was an Indian; it would not look good for her family. I understood.

Another place of entertainment in Kigoma was "The Kigoma Club" in downtown Kigoma, on the waterfront. The club used to be "The English Club" in the colonial days. The "elite" of the town—the district commissioner, the school headmaster, a few expatriates with their wives and a most colorful person, the captain of a riverboat that sailed up and down Lake Tanganyika—frequented it. We gathered there every weekend over beer and gin and tonic to play indoor games such as table tennis, billiards, and badminton. After dark we watched movies displayed by a 35-millimeter projector. The hospital Jeep would pick me up for a ride back to my bungalow at the end of the evening.

Near the end of my one year in Kigoma, in the post-independence, socialist Tanzania, President Nyerere, having a love affair with East Germany, China, and Russia, invited several Chinese doctors to work in our region. There were six sub-specialists, none of whom spoke English, and one translator. We were instructed to teach them our system. They were very friendly and I enjoyed working with them, but a month later I received a notice that my time in Kigoma was over and that I was being transferred to Mpwapwa about half way between Kigoma and Dar-es-Salaam. Although in Mpwapwa I would be happier being closer to my family, I could not help but feel dejected by yet another, what I felt was, act of rejection. The decision was made without my input and it was final. It was an order.

Before I leave speaking of Kigoma, however, I have to give an account of an important case that was to assume great importance later. It happened on a weekend when my parents were visiting me.

A car drove up the dirt road to my bungalow. Out stepped Mr. Fakhru G., the only Bohra man in town, and his very pregnant wife who was obviously in much pain. They told me that she had been in labor for many hours but the baby was stuck. My mom and I got into the car with them and headed to the obstetric ward. On examination I determined that the baby's head had not fully flexed and so I manually flexed it and out popped a healthy baby boy. That event later proved to be another guise in which fortune knocked on my door.

On the hour of my departure from Kigoma, many friends, including the district commissioner, friends from the "English Club," Hosanna's father (Hosanna felt too upset to come), and Fakhru came to wish me good-bye. The district commissioner, knowing my sentiments, urged me not to take it personally. Transferring important people from place to place is how a socialist government keeps a check on insurgency. The socialist politicians suspect that if a man in high position were to stay in a town for long, he could gather a significant following for his political ambitions.

I was angry nonetheless, but after all that I had experienced in Zanzibar, and since the revolution, nothing surprised me anymore. I had learned how to carry on. My focus was the welfare of my parents and family. Nothing else mattered much.

But when the coal engine throbbed and heaved and puffed out of the Kigoma train station that hot afternoon, I wondered when and if I would ever see my loving friends again. I shudder when I think of all that has happened since then. Kigoma and Ujiji, being at the crossroads of the three countries of Congo, Rwanda Burundi, and Tanzania, experienced the highest rates of HIV and AIDS after I left.

Parents visiting Kigoma

Hosanna and friends

Kigoma Hospital

Livingston Monument

With Nursing Staff at Mpwapwa

8

Mpwapwa

MPWAPWA IS A SMALL RURAL town along the railroad, half way between Dar-es-Salaam and Kigoma. Having passed through it, I had taken no notice. But it did not take me long to adapt to the life, work and community there; after all it was just another small town in rural Africa like Kigoma. I made friends quickly with the staff at the hospital and with people in town.

However my boss here was different from my boss in Kigoma. My boss in Kigoma had been not only my mentor but also a friend. My boss in Mpwapwa was a handsome, young African man with a film actor's smile showing brilliant white teeth; he was a smooth talker and very charismatic; but his fake smile put me on guard. I suspected he was not going to be easy to work with.

Of all the places that were available for government employees, he gave me a house two miles away from the hospital; this meant walking two miles each way, in the hot sun, at lunch break. He invented all sorts of excuses when I made a request for a closer place.

I felt lonely and unwanted for a while but soon I found comfort and escape in my work. I was very busy but I enjoyed it. I quickly gained the trust and respect of the staff. Very soon they started confiding in me, for they did not like the boss either. They informed me that he had been trained in Russia and that (from what they had observed) he did not know much medicine. They also told me that for all emergencies he was asking them to fetch me, although the arrangement was for the two of us to alternate weekly calls.

The most frightening discovery I made was when he was on vacation for two weeks and I occupied his office. One day, while searching for something, opening one of the drawers in his desk, I was amazed to find folders with names of some prominent people in the town. The information contained in those pages was not medical at all; it was about where they lived, places they frequented, and with whom they associated. I shared this information with some close friends and it was then that they pointed out to me that in Mpwapwa, every third person is a government informant and that I should be cautious about what I say and with whom I associate.

Feeling uncomfortable in such an environment, I decided to request a transfer to a town closer to Dar-es-Salaam. But my family convinced me that I should leave Tanzania altogether, to pave the way for the family. The future of Indians in East Africa was bleak.

It was very hard for me to think of turning my back on patients such as Maria, a young schoolteacher in labor for four days, who had to travel twenty-five miles on country roads to reach the hospital, arriving on a Saturday in the late evening hours. I was at a local pub in Mpwapwa. The hospital jeep came to fetch me for the emergency. After a quick evaluation it was clear that she had an obstructed labor due to cephalo-pelvic disproportion and as hard as I tried, I could not hear any fetal heartbeat. So I informed her that she needed a Cesarean Section to get the baby out and that the baby was probably dead.

Overnight we made preparations for a C-Section in the morning. We started collecting blood for transfusion if the need arose. Promptly in the early morning we performed the surgery. The amniotic fluid was heavily meconium-stained, which meant the baby had been in great distress. But to everyone's ecstatic surprise the baby was very alive and it was a boy. The messiness of the surgery led to infection and delayed healing of the abdominal wound, requiring the little family to stay in the hospital for several months. They became our favorite patients in the ward.

About two months after their discharge, after working-hours, I heard a knock on my door. It was Maria, her infant and her mother. They said they had come to pay me a visit so that I could check the mother and child. (They were sorry they could not get to the hospital earlier due to difficult travelling conditions.) Being delighted to see them again, I invited them into my house and I carried out the examination in my bedroom. Both mother and child were very well, I informed them. Then they brought forth a large basket of eggs as a present for me. I thanked them for their generosity.

After a brief silence that made me a little uncomfortable, Maria added that that was not the only gift they had brought. I looked but I could not see anything else among their belongings. Then she asked me to guess the name of her child. After my few guesses proved me wrong, she came to my rescue and said it was "Hassanali," which was my official name before I became an American citizen in 1976. I could not hold back my tears of joy and gratitude. The little family had come all the way through twenty-five miles of difficult African territory just to say "thank you."

Experiences of this nature, whereby every little thing I did for the people I served was rewarded with wonderful words of praise and gratitude, made me feel like the hero athlete described by the Greek poet Pindar. One day I discovered my father copied this verse onto one of his little, hidden-away pieces of paper. He quoted:

He who wins of a sudden some noble prize
In the rich years of youth
Is raised high with hopes, his manhood takes wings;
He has in his heart what is better than wealth.
But brief is the season of man's delight
Soon it falls to the grounds;
Some dire decision uproots it.
Thing of a day! Such is man; a shadow in a dream.
Yet when God-given splendor visits him
A bright radiance plays over him, and how sweet is life.

Everyone around me inflated my ego, as did everything I did and enjoyed doing. The world was my oyster. I could have anything I wanted without anyone's help, least of all the help of my childhood God of Zanzibar. I had forgotten Him.

The plan to leave Mpwapwa and Tanzania made me feel very sad and guilty but I had to do it for the welfare of my parents, my siblings and their children.

Through communication with an agency in Rochester, New York, I obtained an internship in Danbury, Connecticut, starting on June 1, 1971. Unfortunately this was very short notice. I did not even have a valid passport. But it so happened that Mr. Fakhru G., who never forgot how I had helped his wife in childbirth, came to visit me in Mpwapwa on his way to Dar-es-Salaam. When I mentioned to him my intention to leave the country and my dilemma of not having a valid passport, he told me he might be able to help me, but that I would have to go to Kigoma with him when he passed by on his way back from Dar-es-Salaam. He kept his promise, picked me up on his way back, secretly met with his "friend" and had a passport made for me.

Now that I had a valid travel document, I took a few weeks of vacation and went to Dar-es-Salaam. First of June had passed, which meant that I had lost my internship position in Danbury. But I was not worried or afraid. I was now bent on leaving for the United States. I made rapid plans to fly to New York and try my luck at another institution. In the first week of July, I boarded a plane. I informed my boss, the medical director in Mpwapwa that I would be on vacation for a month.

My parents, siblings and a few friends came to the airport to see me take off. I hugged and did the salaam greeting to each of them. When my father took my hand, he asked me to forgive him if he had made any mistakes in raising me. This is a standard message of parting in my culture, but I choked up, not believing what I had just heard.

My father's words ring in my head to this day. How could my most loving father, my teacher, my mentor, my friend ever have thought of uttering those precious words? I kissed him, hugged him, ran up the stairs to the plane and buried my face in my hands.

9

New York

THE PLANE LANDED ON JULY 4, 1971. I stayed with a Tanzanian Bohra friend, Mohammed Bhaiji, in Jamaica, New York. Since my internship position was no longer open for me in Connecticut, I went to several hospitals in the city and inquired about an opening. There were none. Not knowing what to do next, I decided to return to Tanzania, to my job in Mpwapwa. To give up so easily would be a mistake, my friend advised; they don't want Indians in East Africa any more, he pointed out. Realizing how right he was, I paid heed to his advice and decided to travel to Rochester, New York, to talk to the agency people who had found me the Danbury position.

After renting a room at the YMCA, I walked around town until I located the office on the second floor of a two-story building, a tiny office with two people, and hardly room to swing a cat. They knew of two openings: one in South Carolina and one in a suburb of Chicago. Since I knew neither place, I asked them to choose one for me. They chose Chicago. So from the YMCA in Rochester, I boarded a Greyhound bus and found my way to Gottlieb Memorial Hospital, a small community hospital in Maywood, Illinois. The beautiful scenery of vast open farms, pasture, and fallow land symbolized a country of infinite opportunities.

At the entrance of the hospital I met a tall pretty woman and a tall man in street clothes with a stethoscope hanging around his neck. They asked if they could help me. I said I had come for my internship and that I was supposed to meet with a Dr. Portes. They paused a little, stared at each other, and then escorted me to Dr. Portes' office. His secretary asked my name and then disappeared for what seemed like a long time.

Upon returning she asked me to step into Dr. Portes' office. Dr. Portes, a clean-shaven, soft-spoken, polite, elderly Greek man with white hair, wearing a blue doctor's coat, stood up, shook my hand, and invited me to sit and relax. He asked me what had brought me there. After I finished explaining, in his fatherly, gentle voice, he informed me that I had shown up a year too early! He said that the internship program at that hospital was not to begin until June, 1972.

I do not recall my reaction but he came to my rescue immediately. I was not to worry, he comforted me, there was plenty of work at the hospital and he would keep me quite busy, working as an employee. Until I found a place to stay, I could even put up in one of the call rooms used by the moonlighting doctors. I did just that and in the morning, promptly at seven a.m., I reported to the office of the head nurse, the tall pretty woman I had met at the entrance the previous day.

After a brief in-service, I was scurrying from room to room, across corridors, and over many floors, starting IV's, inserting catheters, taking histories and performing physicals, doing "scut" work in hospital jargon, oblivious of the doctors and nurses around me. In between being fetched, I would go up to the call room and chat with the moonlighting physicians, doctors who were called to work at the hospital when the need arose. I watched baseball with them, a game new to me.

One of the moonlighters, Dr. Orig, a surgical resident, the tall doctor I had met at the entrance upon my arrival, who said he was from the Philippines (the first Filipino I had met) took a fancy to me. He observed that I was wasting my time doing scut work at the hospital, and encouraged me to go to Chicago and visit all the many hospitals there. I was bound to find an opening, he said.

The logistics of traveling to the city and breaking my contract with Dr. Cesar Portes, who had created a new position for me, dissuaded me from doing that. However, Dr. Orig persisted and invited me to go with him to the city and stay with him for as long as was necessary. Dr. Portes did not object, so I went. Dr. Orig had a great apartment in a big black tower at Navy Pier.

None of the big hospitals in downtown Chicago had any openings. So I ventured farther north. Finally I found an opening at Illinois Masonic Hospital where I was advised to meet with Dr. Iglitsen the next morning. I reported to the office at the time of my appointment and Julie, his secretary, was kind enough to offer me coffee and a pastry she called a doughnut. She sat with me and allayed my anxiety by warning me that Dr. Iglitsen was always late, that I should not worry. A Dr. Chen from China had not shown up for the internship and that I stood a good chance of landing the job.

Sure enough, although very late, Dr. Iglitsen did arrive, rushing into the office, looking excited and very apologetic.

He said he was sorry but that he had been very busy getting ready for his trip. Courteously I asked him where he was going. "Israel," he said; it was his first trip there. I volunteered that he was in for a great treat, for Israel was a very exciting country. I went on describing it, the landscape as well as the culture and he just sat there listening without interruption to all I was saying. When I finished, he asked when I had been there. I said never, but I knew all this from having read the book *Exodus* on my journey from Dar-es-Salaam! We both broke out laughing and then he offered me the position, starting the next day, without even asking me about my medical background. He proudly took me around and introduced me to all the section chiefs. We were both touched by this brief encounter. We bonded. That book was yet another face of good fortune in my life.

When I look back at my initial days in the United States, I cannot help but marvel at how, in the span of one week, my spirit had risen from the feeling of rejection in my own country to one of acceptance and welcome by total strangers in a strange country.

10
Early Years

WHEREAS THE PROFESSIONAL YEARS OF internship and residency were the most fun and memorable years of my life in Chicago, they were also the years of much anguish and personal conflict for me.

For one thing there was not a single soul from Zanzibar or East Africa in my immediate surroundings to guide me or to strike up a friendship with, and not knowing much about the American culture or character, I did not know how to choose friends. I gained some insight from Dale Carnegie books on how to navigate amongst my acquaintances and colleagues at work.

Some American ways of conduct are very different from ours at home. In America, for example, when greeting someone, it is not polite to look down. One should make direct eye contact with the person you are greeting. At home, the opposite is the case. It is a sign of respect to greet with a slight flexion of the neck with the eyes staring down. In

America to be aggressive is a sign of having the potential of a successful person. At home, being gentle and non-aggressive are signs of being a wise and good person.

In addition to feeling lonely, my depressed but curious mind began to notice many ugly and disturbing aspects of American life. The wastefulness of a throw-away consumer society, the built-in obsolescence of American products, the plight of the lonely elderly discarded by society and their children, the corruption of government officials including even governors and presidents, the decadence of drug abuse and violence. Furthermore, in the hospital I began to observe how the practice of medicine, far from being noble, had deteriorated into an industry; how, for example, poor girls on public aid were coerced into undergoing hysterectomies when according to my books, given their diagnoses, there were no good indications for such a drastic procedure. Schumacher's *Small is Beautiful*, Frederick Turner's *Beyond Geography*, De Tocqueville's *Democracy in America* are some of the books that became my bedfellows in the dark nights.

I needed to connect with something, someone, anyone. I started looking for a Bohra community. My parents had informed me that there was a prince, a son of our Maulana, who was living in Chicago. I found him in the Yellow Pages, called him, and he invited me to his house. I met him at the entrance where he stood talking to someone. He was on his way out but he greeted me and then invited me to meet him at evening prayers.

The small Bohra community met in a rented hall. I left early that afternoon, taking the bus and then the train to meet people on time, with the hope of making connections. There were a handful of people there but no one spoke to me. Finally the *Bhai sahib*, the prince, came. We all prayed together. When the prayers were over, everyone wrapped up their prayer mats and left, including the prince. I stood on my mat alone, rather disappointed and a little shocked that the Bhai-sahib did not remember me from that morning or if he did, he did not bother to talk to me. I walked away from the hall feeling no interest in returning.

The next morning, having no other way of coping with my life situation, I resolved to immerse myself in my duties and work as a rotating intern. Fully attending to my work selflessly had always made me feel good. It also made me feel connected with the community I served. It was my new religion. I got busy learning new concepts and technologies; I attended weekend staff parties and established new friendships. I even ate all my meals at the hospital and rented an apartment a few blocks away. Illinois Masonic Hospital became my school, my community, my playground and my sanctuary.

I never thought of my Bohra community, never prayed and never thought of Allah. Praying, repeating rituals almost thoughtlessly, without understanding, had become unrewarding. It was like putting money in a bank that did not exist. I ignored all those letters from home, from people asking me to sponsor them so they could migrate to the U.S. They would not have believed me if I had advised them to think of somewhere else to go. They would not have believed that "all that glitters is not gold," my father's frequent refrain, is true, because to live where and how I lived was not easy.

After my internship, I continued as an Internal Medicine resident at Illinois Masonic Hospital and in my final year, having gained the trust and respect of my teachers, I was appointed as one of the chief residents in the program.

It was then that I met Mary.

Some of the Daleys and in-laws

11

Mary

MARY AND I MET AT my hospital where she had a job in the Social Work department.

As a senior resident, in charge of sometimes very ill patients who required much assistance after their discharge from the hospital—some to nursing homes and some to their own home where often there was no one to help them—I came to know the staff in her department very well. Very often we would have lunch together in the cafeteria. They were a fun group, very intelligent, very professional, with a high regard for the welfare of the patient. And since they did not wear uniforms like nurses did, they looked very pretty.

Mary was the prettiest, the most lively, with a great sense of humor, an easy smile and great dimples. One day we found each other at lunch, just the two of us. I talked to her about a very moving book I had been reading then, *Bury My Heart at Wounded Knee*. She told me she had already read it and loved it. I was very impressed.

She refused to go out on a date with me the first time I asked her; she had never gone out with a foreign person before. But she did agree the second time and when we parted that evening, I felt as if I had been struck with a magic wand. The last time I had felt like that was with Hosanna in Kigoma.

We became an item after that first date. She brought me into her circle of fun-loving, wonderful friends all of whom are still our best friends, and her family who embraced me and came to love me as one of their own. A year after we met, we decided to get married, and I wrote to my parents about my intention. My father wrote back, not saying I should not go ahead with it, but that I should think carefully about it. Cultural differences can create difficulties in a marriage. But I was bent on leaving the institution of my childhood; I did not mind crossing cultures. My childhood institution had broken my heart in several ways even though it had nurtured the child in me so lovingly and I had loved it very much. To be married outside it was a final stamp on my desire to cross over.

Mary and I were married on a beach across from our apartment on East Lake Terrace in Chicago, not far from where we live now. Mary wore a flowing, white dress and I wore a tan suit tailored in Zanzibar. An Episcopalian minister, a friend of her brother Dan, married us. Dan's friend, Terry Rynne, sang the song "Bridge over Troubled Waters" and a handful of friends from work celebrated with us over wine and cold cut sandwiches. A few onlookers watched us from a beautiful sailing boat on the calm turquoise waters of Lake Michigan, bathed in the soft golden glow of a setting September sun.

That day Mary rescued me out of a rudderless, capsizing boat, as it were. She was as bright as she was pretty, she was as alive as she was friendly, and she was the guiding star in my life. That day I was launched on an exciting chapter of an eventful life.

Suddenly and surprisingly, my old god of Zanzibar resurfaced in my life, dressed in Christian clothes.

Mary has five sisters and one brother, Dan Daley, a priest. At about the time I appeared on the scene and after he struck up a close friendship with an ex-nun, Sheila, who later became his wife, Dan dropped out of the priesthood due to disagreement with the policies of the Catholic Church. But because both he and Sheila were very committed to the Catholic community, they were determined to launch a reform organization they named "Call to Action."

Such a grand venture required a great deal of preparation. A facet of this preparation required studying other counter movements so they formed a study group which met every week to study the Bible, liberation theology which grew out of Central American Christianity, Christian mystics and even Gandhi who had been much influenced by Christian thought.

The timing of this could not have been better for me. Like Dan and Sheila, I had also grown up in a very religious environment and like them I was also having a conflict with my religion. I was eager to learn the ways of other religions and explore the real meaning of religious thought.

We met every week. The meeting started with a previously assigned reading from the Bible, a period of meditation on the reading, followed by a discussion. We explored the history of Christianity and its impact on the world. We also studied the life of Gandhi and learned how his political life was influenced not only by the Bhagavad Gita (the Hindu scripture) but also by Christianity. We worked on improving our meditation skills, which led me to explore Buddhism and the life and teachings of the Buddha.

Our group and our explorations became a much-needed spiritual sanctuary for me at a time when I had entered this new phase of my life. I had finished my residency but had not decided what sort of medical practice I was going to establish. Mary had a job but now we had two beautiful children. Wishing to spend as much time as we could with our children, neither of us wanted to work full time. So Mary worked half time and I did part time work in different clinics just to make enough money to get by.

But that left me with no steady work environment and no team. (I like to work with a team.) Moreover being busy with two babies left Mary and me with less time for each other and that caused me some stress too. So our religious study group and meditation practices could not have come at a better time in my life; they helped me center myself.

As I said, we studied the history of Christianity. To learn that it was rooted in the political struggles of the poor population of Judea was a mind-changing experience for me. I had never thought of religions in that light before.

At the time Jesus was born, Judea was ruled by the Roman Emperor Octavius who had been anointed by the Roman Senate as a god, to be worshipped as a god by the whole Roman Empire. The Romans were ruthless. They levied heavy taxes on their subjects in Judea and controlled them with the iron hand of Governor Herod, a cruel and ruthless man in his own right. The Emperor had chosen him from among the Judeans. Herod was born a Jew, and he appointed the high priests of the Jews as his helpers. The high priests in their turn subjugated and controlled the masses through the creation of rules and regulations that were humiliating, unjust and impoverishing. This led to much unrest in Judea. Crime and killing, especially of the rich, were rampant. People were ready for a violent uprising, but Jesus, discerning that violence against an empire like Rome would be suicidal, proposed a new order based on love, equality and brotherhood. He also developed a nonviolent strategy for dealing with the unjust superpower. His success in gathering support threatened the priests and the Governor so much so that they had to crucify him.

This theory of the origin of Christianity explained the success of the religious movement to me. It was a grass roots socio-political movement. It made sense.

As I thought about it further, I began to see its similarity to Gandhiji's nonviolent struggles against the British Empire, and his support of the untouchables in the Hindu caste system. In the same vein, the Buddha, the founder of Buddhism, emerges as a social revolutionary pointing out the injustice built into that caste system. He claimed that a person born in the soldier caste cannot call himself a soldier unless he was a soldier by trade; or a Brahmin cannot call himself a Brahmin unless he practices priesthood and so on.

Suddenly the boundaries between politics and religion were beginning to fade in my mind and in some strange way I was feeling empowered to think freely, free of any fear of being called a heretic.

The most important circumstance was that I could read the Bible and understand it. I knew English (even though it was not the original language in which it was written). It is not full of verses I memorized and repeated in prayers, the way I recited the Qur'an; the Bible's verses I tried to understand and apply to my life and psyche in order to gain peace and happiness. This was very different from reading the Qur'an whose language I did not understand at all.

I will never forget the first time I felt a shift in my mind, my heart and my person. It was when we were studying St. Paul's first letter to the Corinthians in which, in chapter 13, he speaks of love; that love is kind, love is not jealous or selfish, etc. I felt a palpable shift, like when the ground shifts in a landslide or when the effect of a tranquilizer kicks in and the body's tension dissipates or when the high temperature of a fever drops to normal.

I understood love, not like that for a lover or a child or a job, but like a love one feels for vulnerable mute life, or the love Jesus felt for his executioners, or Gandhiji felt for the British who imprisoned him, or the love some parents have reported they felt for the gunman who shot their only child. Once I got it, I felt it deep within my bones. It became part of my chemistry and it felt wonderful. I had come to understand the difference between materialistic love and spiritual love.

A religious teaching had transformed my orientation to life. This happened because I read the passage and meditated on it as if it were written for me. I read it with my heart rather than with my head. I felt as if I had broken a secret code. From then on I always read things that way, with my heart. Not only that, but I think that since then I have learnt to see, hear and even speak with my heart. I remember Jesus saying somewhere that if you keep knocking at a door long enough it will eventually break open. I think a door of my heart broke open that day at our meeting. After all, I had been searching for God for a long time.

12

Christian Sojourn

AROUND THIS TIME IN MY life, I had persuaded my younger sister Gulshan and her husband to migrate to the USA. They had arrived in 1978. Since their arrival they had managed to locate and join the growing Bohra community in Chicago. Even though it was far from my house, I went with them to keep in touch with the larger community. However, after a year or so I once again became disappointed. The socialization was fun but the time spent driving to the mosque and sitting in the mosque was too long. My work and family life kept me very busy.

I was enjoying my new religious discoveries. Our little family started going to a Presbyterian church on Sundays. We lived in Wilmette then, near Mary's mother. I enjoyed the sermons of the minister Robert Lee, a very learned, thoughtful and charming man with a big heart. I enjoyed how he weaved the lessons of the scriptural readings of the day in and out of his or other parishioners' life experiences.

When we moved to Evanston after our second and third children—Jehan and Joseph—were born, I started frequenting the Lake Street Church of Evanston. This is a non-denominational church although in the past it had been a Baptist church. I loved learning about the Baptist denomination. A person gets baptized in adulthood, after much thought and study. One can decide not to be a Baptist even though the rest of the family may be. Moreover each Baptist congregation is fully in charge of its agenda and finances, independent of all other congregations. This was very different from what I knew about religions. I could see the American democratic free spirit at work in the Baptist Church community.

The most significant aspect of the Lake Street Church was the minister, Robert Thompson, also a very charming, learned and compassionate man. Most of all he was interested in all the religions of the world and he prided himself on being called a Buddhist-Baptist minister! His sermons were also very relevant to life experiences. With time we struck up a close friendship. I learnt much from him about Buddhist thought and I taught him a little about Islam.

At this juncture, however, I have to make a confession. Having grown up in an Islamic culture, having followed the dictates of the religion for years, having prayed in mosques for years, repeating the same words without knowing their meaning, and feeling short-changed for not having been taught the language that we read and prayed in, I felt a little discontented with Islam and therefore did not pay any attention to Islamic literature when we were studying Christianity, Hinduism and Buddhism. I had set aside my copy of the "Al Qur'an," the Muslim bible, which Muslims claim contains the words of God passed on to us by the Prophet Mohammed. I did come to it in the end, but much later.

It was around this time that I felt a second shift occur within me. It was when I met Susan, a human resources manager of a powdered-paint manufacturing plant in Paterson, New Jersey. At that time I had found work with a group of "environmental physicians." I was sent by the group to perform "surveillance physical examinations" of workers to detect work-related health problems. Since neither Susan nor I was clear about how to carry out the project, we decided to meet for dinner to plan how we were going to organize it. Susan knew a chef at a small restaurant with four or five tables in a farmhouse on the outskirts of the town. It was small, quiet, dimly lit and quaint, perfect for good conversation.

Susan, although Jewish, was a strict vegetarian. She ordered a beautifully presented broad slice of fried tofu with colorful vegetables. I ordered fried chicken or catfish, I forget.

Since it took a while to be served our meals, by the time they arrived, we were clear about how we were going to carry out our project. We were able to concentrate and enjoy our meals fully. While I was eating (and I am quite slow when it comes to eating), I happened to notice how Susan was eating. She was slow, quiet, methodical, careful and almost prayerful. And as I kept watching, I felt my mind's eye shift to a scene many decades ago in our small house on Saxi Street in Zanzibar, with my parents and siblings sitting on the floor around a large metal plate, our heads covered, picking our food carefully with our fingers. That scene and the present scene of Susan eating had in common an atmosphere of reverence, gratitude, and humility—the food was handled as if it were sacred. Struck by how long it had been since I had felt like this at a simple dinner table awakened in me the realization that I had been living so fast a life that I was not paying attention to detail—the beauty, the magic and the sanctity of all that is. That day I resolved to observe the world with a more loving and admiring eye rather than a critical and ungrateful one. Rituals gained a higher value.

13

Islam

AFTER THIS ENCOUNTER, IN LATE 1986, I went to visit my family in Dar-es-Salaam. It was a perfect time to sit down with my father and discuss Islam with him, a learned, unassuming, well-rounded, loving man, content with the simple pleasures of life, highly respected and loved in the community, and a devout Muslim. When I asked him how much Islam had influenced him, he said he could not separate his self from Islam, that a prayerful life in community, following the principles of the seven pillars of Islam, can lead a person to become angelic and achieve contentment and happiness. He went on to explain the seven "pillars" of *Wallayat* (love), *Tahaarat* (purity), *Salaat* (prayers), *Zakaat* (taxes), *Saum* (fasting), *Haj* (pilgrimage) and *Jihaad* (fighting, or striving to improve oneself), a word whose meaning unfortunately has been much adulterated by politicians.

On my return to Chicago from Dar-es-Salaam, my boss, whose son had just finished his residency in Internal

Medicine, gave me two weeks' notice to resign. He calculated that he did not need, nor could afford, to pay two internists in the group. He preferred to have his son work for him, not me. Although at first I was angry and upset with him, this insult turned out to be a blessing. It drove me to look for another job. My search landed me in a large industrial clinic where I made friends with a Hindu orthopedic surgeon, Dr. Ashok Ray.

On my desk at the clinic, I kept a framed "OHM," written in Sanskrit. It is the Hindu symbol of God. One day it fell on its side and I saw it on the floor, lying sideways. In that way, in Arabic, it read "Allah," the Muslim name for God! (See below.)

I was taken aback by this. I shared this discovery with Ashok. Since he knew of my interest in such matters, and since he had just returned from Calcutta after his father's death, accompanied by a Hindu nun to help him grieve, he invited me to talk to her over dinner. She was a professor of Sanskrit at the University of Calcutta and her expertise was in the Bhagavad Gita. Over a vegetarian dinner, I asked *Mashima* (auntie)—for that is what everyone endearingly called her—to summarize for me what the Gita teaches about the goal of life and how to attain it. She explained that humans suffer because of our separation from God and to cope with suffering we should strive to return to God, become one with God. To attain such a union we should observe a practice of the following principles: *Austium* (non-stealing, which also means being grateful for our indebtedness to God, parents, teachers and other living things because they all help us to be alive), *Sochun* (purity), *Ahimsa* (nonviolence), *Sanjam*, (restraint) and *Satyam* (truth).

Hearing this and recognizing its similarity to Islamic philosophy, I was amazed; it was almost unbelievable because heretofore I had thought Hinduism and Islam to be incompatible. I had been basing that assumption on social values rather than philosophical ones. Hindus do not eat meat; they worship the cow; Muslims eat meat and slaughter the cow. Drinking alcohol and gambling are considered sinful in Islam, not so in Hinduism, and so on. To my surprise, I was discovering the same philosophy in the two religions. Huxley calls it "*The Perennial Philosophy.*"

So I started to study the history of Islam and quickly discovered the political underpinning of Prophet Muhammad's life. Mecca, when he was a child, was a metropolitan trading center at the cross roads of several caravan routes. It was ruled by an oligarchy that included the Quraish, his clan, his relatives. But there was a big gap between the rich and the poor. The poor, the widows and the orphans had no one looking after them. The Prophet's own mother was already a widow when he was born and he became an orphan at the age of six years.

The Arabs living in the desert lived in separate marauding tribal groups and each tribe had its own God. Arabia in those times was wild and uncivilized. Whereas all their neighbors (the Jews, the Christians and the Persians, whom the Prophet met on his travels as a caravan driver in his youth) had a religion and a Book to guide them in how to live peacefully and how to take care of society as a whole, the Arabs had no such Book or common religion.

The Prophet's studies, meditations and prayers culminated in a series of revelations which, many years after his death, were compiled into the book called *Al Qur'an*, the Muslim equivalent of the Bible and a book of law. The rituals built around it brought Muslims together and created a civilization unmatched by any other in human history. It brought new vitality to a stagnant world and transformed it forever.

Like Christianity and Buddhism, Islam too was a socio-political-religious movement at its inception. Whereas Jesus emerged as a spiritual teacher and philosopher, (like Socrates did four hundred years before him in Athens), sacrificing his life by challenging the Emperor's claim that the emperor was God, Mohammed arose as a spiritual teacher and a successful statesman, like Hammurabi did twenty centuries before him in Babylon. While Hammurabi wrote down the first book of law for Babylon (first of its kind in human history), Mohammed brought Al Qur'an to the Arabs, a first book of scripture for them. I was thrilled to think of Mohammed and Islam in this light.

I then resolved to read the Bhagavad Gita and Al Qur'an side by side in order to examine and compare the philosophies. It did not take long to find common concepts of God, Good, Evil, Heaven and Hell, and the concept of Avatar, the descent of God's messenger on earth in times of irreligiosity. Playfully, I even noted similarities in words; for example, "Rahman" is "Brahman" without a "B" or "Sura" is "Sutra" without a "T"; and ALIF (A), LAM (L), MEEM (M), letters that are considered mysterious, written at the beginning of many Qur'anic chapters, when mouthed as a word can sound like "ALM or OHM"! As a result, my view of Islam assumed a much deeper meaning than I had known growing up as a Muslim.

In all my religious learning during my childhood, the emphasis was on rituals and the worship of the Prophet's family and other saints. So, having learned how to read scriptures, from reading the Bible and the Bhagavad Gita, I was now ready to tackle Al Quran even if it meant studying it on my own.

Many very good translations of Al Quran are now

available. I started praying every day—reciting, studying and meditating on the short 30 verses at the end of "Al Qur'an," verses we frequently recite in our prayers. Slowly but surely, I began to understand Qur'an's teachings. I was reading it like I had learnt to read the Bible, with my heart. Soon I began to feel a change occur within me, in my orientation to life and to the world.

It became a thrill to watch the sun break the day in the east, to see the birds rise in the sky, hear them sing in the cool breeze, and pray:

> "Al hamdo lillahe Rbbiul Aalameen"-
> Praise be to the Creator of the Universe —
> (for all this magic I am witnessing),
>
> "Arrahmaanir Rrahim" - God the Gracious and the Merciful — Guide me through this day to strive for the greater good, Not just my good or some other individual's.
>
> Guide me on the right path, not the path of those who are led astray.

A Muslim recites this verse thirteen times a day, as a "dhikre"— a reminder, to stay the course at every moment.

I had heard Christians recite a very similar prayer, the Lord's Prayer:

> Our Father who art in heaven
> Hallowed be thy name
> Thy Kingdom come
> Thy will be done
> On earth as it is in heaven

85

> Give us this day our daily bread
> And forgive us our debts
> As we also have forgiven our debtors
> And lead us not into temptation
> But deliver us from evil.

I find these prayers very similar. Both of them emphasize the greatness of the Creator, both pray for God's help in devoting our lives to the service of God's creation (for the greater good, not our selfish greed), and both pray for help in avoiding evil.

I was not surprised for long because in the chapter entitled Surat'al Ibrahim, I read "We sent not any messenger but with the tongue of his folk in order that he make manifest for them," meaning that every civilization has its own sacred text so that people can learn how to live happily from studying their own scripture written in a language that they can understand.

The biggest discovery was that Al Qur'an and Bhagavad Gita are very similar. All my life I had been told otherwise, in fact we were discouraged from reading Bhagavad Gita. I felt like screaming with joy at this find. I could not wait to share it with Bohras and Hindus. I wrote a paper on my finding and showed it to the editor of an Indian newspaper in Chicago but he did not show any interest. I even showed it to a board of a Hindu temple, but again there was no interest there. I gave copies to my family members and that is as far as it went. I wondered if people were fearful of publicizing such a find.

But here are a few examples of what I am talking about. People can explore them on their own:

On the nature of the prophets, in Qur'an, Chapter 2, verse 136, it is written:

We believe in Allah and (in) that which has been revealed to us,

and (in) that which was revealed to Ibrahim and Ismail and Ishaq

and Yaqoub and the Tribes, and in that which was given to Musa

and to Isa and in that which was given to the Prophets from their Lord;

we do not make distinction between any of them, and to Him do we submit."

In Chapter 2, verse 213, it is written:

...all people are a single nation; so Allah raised prophets as bearers of good news and as warners, and He revealed them the Book with truth.

In the Bhagavad Gita, in Chapter 4, text 7, Shri Krishna pronounces to Arjun:

Whenever and wherever there is a decline in religious practice, Oh descendent of Bharat, and a predominant rise of irreligion, at that time I descend myself.

On the nature of God and His closeness to us, Chapter 50, verse 16 of Al Qur'an, I found:

And certainly We created Man and We know what his mind suggests to him, and We are nearer to him than his life-vein.

Similarly, in the Bhagavad Gita in Chapter 7, Text 10, Shri, Krishna says:

> The Supreme Lord is situated in every-one's heart, Oh Arjuna, and is directing the wanderings of all living entities, who are seated on a machine, made of the material energy."

In Chapter 10, Text 20, Krishna says again:

> I am the Self seated in the hearts of all creatures. I am the beginning, the middle and the end of all beings.

I could not stop digging deeper and deeper into the night while my family slept. The more I dug, the more pearls showed up on many topics concerning our orientation and approach to life.

On the subject of duty, and the goals of one's efforts in life, in Al Quran, in Chapter 4, verse 74 I read the famous lines for which non-Muslims, not understanding the metaphor, criticize Islam:

> Therefore let those fight in the way of Allah, who sell this world's life for the hereafter; and whoever fights in the way of Allah, then be he slain or be he victorious, we shall grant him a mighty reward.

And lo and behold, In Bhagavad Gita, in Chapter 3, Text 30, Krishna pronounces:

> Therefore Arjun, surrendering all your works to Me, with mind and intent on Me,

without desire for gain and free of egoism
and lethargy, fight.

Both passages implore us to realize that each of us has, within us, a tendency to do good and a tendency to do bad. These tendencies are constantly at war with each other within us. We have to fight the evil forces in order to bring forth the good in us.

On the concept of God as light, in another famous chapter, Chapter 11, Text 13 of the Gita, Krishna says:

If hundreds of thousands of suns rose
up at once into the sky, they might resem-
ble the effulgence of the Supreme Person in
that universal form.

In Al Qur'an, in Chapter 24, verse 35, it is written:

God is the Light of the heavens and the
earth.
The parable of His Light
Is a niche in which there is a lamp.
The lamp is in a glass.
The glass is as if it had been a glittering
star
Kindled from a blessed olive tree,
Neither eastern nor western,
Whose oil of the olive is about to illu-
minate
Although no fire touches it.

I can go on and on for a long time, pick every topic in life and show how similar the philosophies of Islam and

Hinduism are. I think the same is true for Christianity, Judaism and Islam. I found similarity even with Buddhism even though to the Buddha, to achieve happiness, a belief in the concept of God is not relevant.

Take for example one of the fundamental concepts of Buddhism, the concept of contingency, of "conditioned arising," which claims that all phenomena in the universe are evolved from and will cause the evolution of other phenomena, which in turn means that the universe is in a constant state of flux, of change. Nothing is permanent. This property therefore renders everything unreliable as a source of permanent happiness and therefore every phenomenon in the universe is a potential source of anguish and distress if we crave it, get attached to it, because it is bound to change or end. "*Sab be sankhara dukkha*," Buddha pronounced; all life is a potential source of suffering.

But if we understand the true nature of the universe, its illusiveness, we can stop our cravings and desires and get rid of them altogether. By doing that we can perceive and enjoy the true nature of things; we learn to accept life for what it is, with all its challenges caused by change, loss and death. Such an orientation to life will create the platform to live a spiritually rich life according to the Buddha's Eight-Fold Path of right view, right intention, right speech, right action, right livelihood, right effort, right mindfulness, and right concentration.

In Al Quran this whole concept is succinctly put in Chapter 103, called "Al Asr."

It is commonly translated as:

> Throughout the passage of Time, hu-
> man beings are lost, except those who have
> the right belief, do righteous deeds, those

> who remind others of truth and reality, and
> those who remind others to be patient with
> each other.

The word *asr* is translated as "passage of time" but it has many meanings. It literally means to squeeze (like squeezing grapes), to press, to wring, a whirlwind, a hurricane as well as "succession of ages." In my mind all these words echo the Buddhist concept of contingency, change, flux and impermanence. The word could also connote that humans are "trapped" and confined, squeezed within themselves by their self-serving egos.

Then it says humans are "lost." Lost where? Lost from the path of happiness is what I think it says. Lost due to greed, hatred and craving for worldly things, unless they believe. Believe what? Believe in the faith of Islam. And what does Islam mean? It means to submit to the ways of God, the ways of the universe, by realizing the reality and the truth of what the universe is: illusive. And what does submit mean? To me it means to accept graciously, patiently, without resistance, to see it for what it is. Such an orientation will lead us to understand life truthfully and lead us to a rich, spiritual path of life, laid down by the seven pillars of Islam that my father talked about.

In Buddhist cosmology there is a demon called Mara. The Wikipedia definition of Mara is that it personifies unwholesome impulses, unskillfulness, and the death of the spiritual life. He is a temper, distracting humans from practicing the spiritual life by making mundane things alluring or the negative seem positive.

Similarly, in Al Quran, in the last chapter, Chapter 114 called "al-Nas," which means "humanity," we are led to meditate thus:

> I seek refuge with the Lord of Human-
> ity, the sovereign of Humans, the God of
> Humans, from the evil of the whispering
> elusive temper who whispers in the heart
> of Humans — from all [temptations to evil
> invisible forces] as well as from humans."

Al Quran is replete with such wonderful verses written in a beautiful, lyrical language and style. For some reason, the sound of the words has a magical effect on my heart. It may be because I learnt to recite them in my childhood and repeated them millions of times in a reverential environment. They sank into my bones. They have the effect of unfolding me, the effect of uplifting my spirits and calming them. They invite me to allow the world to be what it is, to embrace it for what it is. They remind me of the wonder that is life and celebrate it at every breath.

To use an analogy from baseball, a game I learned during my early days in Chicago, I had a great at-bat, I had run through all the bases, and though covered with dirt and bruises, I was safe at home plate again. I had scored. The whole universe was celebrating. I had no quarrel with anyone anymore.

I cannot end the book without mentioning Rib-hi, a twenty-some-year-old Palestinian boy, as old as my oldest son was at the time. He was an attendant I had come to know at the gas station across the street from our clinic near Midway Airport, far away from my home.

It had been a very busy, snowy, winter day. It was dark when I walked to my car after I closed the clinic, but I could see that one of the tires was flat. Exhausted and dejected, I dragged the car into the gas station and Rib-hi, as usual, greeted me with "*As salaamo alaikum*" and asked me how I was doing. I told him how miserable I was and what a day I had at the clinic and now I had to deal with this!

He listened to me complain and when I finished, with a gentle smile he remarked that I should not feel this way, especially if I was a Muslim. A real Muslim allows and accepts such mishaps, after all that is what the word "Islam" means, a sort of resignation, acceptance, going with the flow no matter what life brings. Accept it, understand it, face it, and take care of it. There was no point in wasting mental energy in frustration, anger and dejection.

It was truly a great lesson from a youngster, a lesson I have never forgotten. Suffering in life is to be expected, as Gautam Buddha preached; the best response is acceptance, not resistance; to do what we have to do, carry out our duty, as Lord Krishna advises Arjun in the battlefield of Kurukshetra; the rest will take care of itself.

Ohm and Allah

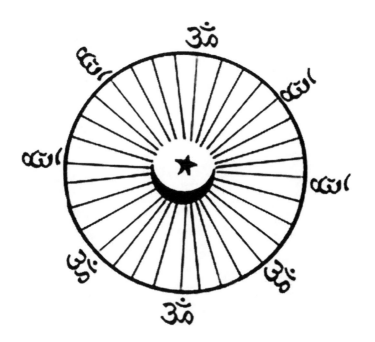

Appendix

Sunni Muslims and Shia Muslims are all followers of Islam, the religion founded by Prophet Muhammed who is considered the sixth Prophet of the Muslims, the first being Adam, followed by Noah, Ibrahim (Abraham), Musa (Moses) and Isa (Jesus).

Sunnis are a majority group of Muslims who believe that the successors of Prophet Muhammed were elected and they were Abubakar, Omar , Othman, and Ali in that order.

Shias believe that the successor of the Prophet was chosen by the Prophet himself and that was Imam Ali his cousin.

Shias are divided into several sects and each sect is an institution led by a spiritual leader whose title is Maulana, akin to the Pope. The Bohras call him Dai also.

The titles of Sheikh and Mullahs are given to people who serve the community in various ways, such as with money, with their time and voluntary work. Study of scriptures was a requirement in the past but it is not so these days.